AF596800

BRONX SOCRATES

BRONX SOCRATES

Portrait of a Legendary Teacher

EDITED BY
STEVEN M. CAHN

RESOURCE *Publications* • Eugene, Oregon

BRONX SOCRATES
Portrait of a Legendary Teacher

Resource Publications
An Imprint of Wipf and Stock Publishers
199 W. 8th Ave., Suite 3
Eugene, OR 97401

www.wipfandstock.com

PAPERBACK ISBN: 979-8-3852-1282-8
HARDCOVER ISBN: 979-8-3852-1283-5
EBOOK ISBN: 979-8-3852-1284-2

07/30/24

With gratitude to all teachers who care deeply about their students and strive to help them succeed.

Contents

PART II. ESSAYS

PART III. WRITINGS

Acknowledgments

I THANK THOSE FORMER students of Bob Gurland who contributed to this collection as well as the estate of Sidney Hook for permission to reprint material from his *Education for Modern Man: A New Perspective.* I am also grateful to Dr. Mary Ann McHugh of Arizona State University for her expert polishing of all the essays.

The source from which most of the chapters in this book are drawn is an unpublished manuscript titled "Unopened Letters: A Festschrift (of Sorts)," designed and developed by attorney Joseph Di Salvo. He spearheaded various celebratory events for his teacher Bob Gurland, and without Joe's efforts this volume would not exist. He is also the producer and director of the documentary film *Bronx Socrates,* available at www. bronxsocrates.com.

Preface

ACADEMIC LIFE REGULARLY HONORS leading scholars but rarely recognizes those professors who have excelled in undergraduate teaching. This book salutes Bob Gurland, a paragon in the classroom who recently retired after having taught over 25,000 college students, first at C.W. Post College, then for many decades at New York University (NYU) and also for several years at the United States Military Academy at West Point. Over that time thousands of those who studied with him have expressed their appreciation for the insights he offered, the care he displayed, and the joy he fostered. In the words of one, echoed by numerous others, "I have had many professors over the course of my education but only one teacher."

To honor him on his ninetieth birthday, his former students were invited to send reminiscences for inclusion in a collection to be presented to him. A few of the many that arrived are offered in Part I of this book. Some contributions took the form of academic essays based on research he inspired, and these are contained in Part II along with a chapter on the good teacher authored by the eminent political philosopher Sidney Hook (1902–1989), who greatly admired Bob's teaching. Although Bob himself published rarely, one essay he wrote has been widely praised, and part of it is included in Part III along with a collection of his memorable aphorisms that students have cherished.

While no writing can replicate the experience of those who attended Bob's classes, my hope is that this book will convey a sense of his commitment to students, the enthusiasm he generated, and the appreciation he engendered.

About Robert H. Gurland

ROBERT H. GURLAND WAS born in 1933 in the Bronx, New York. Following his graduation from the Bronx High School of Science, he attended the City College of New York, where he majored in mathematics and history, earning his bachelor's degree in 1955. While competing in various amateur baseball leagues, he pursued his passion for music, playing trumpet in jazz, swing, and Latin bands, including those fronted by Gene Krupa, Lionel Hampton, and Tito Puente.

Seeking dependable employment, he accepted a position at the Rockefeller Institute, first mastering then managing the cytology department's innovative program in electron microscopy. Once the laboratory was running smoothly, he decided that the time had come to develop his interest in teaching.

Not possessing state certification, he began at the private Eastwoods School in Oyster Bay, Long Island, where he taught fifth and sixth grades, covering all subjects. He then was accepted in a master's program at Adelphi University's School of Education, where in 1959 he earned his degree with a concentration in mathematics and obtained New York State certification to teach the subject at all levels from kindergarten through high school. While at Adelphi, he was encouraged to study philosophy and took two courses at Columbia University, one taught by Joseph Epstein, the other by Sidney Morgenbesser.

At Adelphi his thesis on the pedagogy of mathematics impressed the faculty, who recommended him to the Roslyn, Long Island, school system to teach mathematics at the junior high school and high school levels. He remained there from 1959 to 1963, receiving early tenure in 1960. While in Roslyn, he received a grant from the National Science Foundation (NSF) to spend the summer taking graduate mathematics courses at San Jose State College in California. Subsequently, he received another grant from the NSF to take a leave of absence from the Roslyn schools and remain at San Jose for an additional year.

Having promised to return to Roslyn for at least one year, he did so, but then in 1965 accepted an assistant professorship in the mathematics department at C. W. Post College of Long Island University. There in 1968 he was chosen as The Man of the Year by the Student Government Association and was promoted to associate professor with tenure, staying until 1971. During that time, under the auspices of the NSF, he offered seminars in mathematics to faculty in school districts in the tri-state area.

Meanwhile, he decided that his talents and interests would be better served by teaching philosophy rather than mathematics. As he was working during the day, he enrolled in the philosophy department at NYU, which offered evening courses. He studied primarily with Sidney Hook, William Barrett, Richard Martin, and Milton Munitz, all of whom were enthusiastic about his work. Indeed, on one occasion when Barrett had a medical problem and could attend but not teach the three-hour class, he asked Bob whether he could offer a lecture on the logical system developed by the British idealist philosopher F. H. Bradley. Although Bob knew nothing about that subject, he prepared assiduously, delivered the lecture, was applauded by the students, and gained Barrett's admiration.

In 1968, when Barrett temporarily assumed the Schweitzer Chair at NYU, he had been scheduled to teach a large section of introductory philosophy but was unable to do so. He recommended to Hook, the long-time head of the department, that Bob be given the assignment. Hook agreed, and Bob turned out to be hugely successful with the students. Indeed, they urged that he be given more courses to teach, and by the time Bob completed his doctoral course work and passed his qualifying examinations, he was teaching more students than any member of the NYU department.

Steven Cahn became Bob's dissertation advisor, and in spring 1971 Bob successfully defended his thesis devoted to the problem of induction. Immediately after, Hook offered and Bob accepted a tenure-track assistant professorship.

In 1973 the NYU Alumni Association awarded Bob their Great Teacher Award, making him the youngest and only untenured instructor ever chosen for this honor. He was promoted to associate professor with tenure in 1974 and to full professor two years later. For many years Bob also served the philosophy department as director of undergraduate students and for a ten-year period was department chair.

In 1974 he appeared on the CBS television nationally syndicated show "Sunrise Semester," offering a course in practical reasoning. Because he would conclude each lecture with a logical puzzle, he earned the sobriquet "Dr. Puzzles."

Seven years later he returned to offer a course titled "Experiencing Sport: A Philosophical and Cultural Analysis." That course earned him numerous plaudits, such as that offered by the well-known Newsday sports columnist Stan Isaacs, who wrote, "Robert Gurland is a regular-guy professor of philosophy at NYU who is teaching a course on sports on the Sunrise Semester early morning television show that is one of the best meat-and-potatoes analyses of sports that I have ever come across in the papers, books, or on television."

In 1994 Bob was granted a leave of absence from NYU to serve as a Visiting Professor in Humanities housed in the Department of English at the United State Military Academy at West Point. A cheating scandal had rocked the Academy, and Bob's charge was to initiate a curriculum concerned with ethics and professionalism and prepare faculty to teach the course. The effort was successful, and to this day the course is required of all cadets and is taught by civilian faculty with doctoral degrees.

Bob was invited by the Academy to continue for an additional year during which he taught a section of the ethics course as well as presenting courses titled "Practical Reasoning," "Marx, Freud, and Einstein" and "War and Morality." At the end of that year, he was offered the opportunity to become the first civilian tenured professor in the history of West Point, but he chose to return to NYU. Nevertheless, in 1978 he was awarded the Outstanding Civilian Service Medal by the Department of the Army and the United State Congress, the highest honor that the Department can offer a civilian.

Even after his return to NYU, Bob remained a frequent guest at West Point. He was also an invited speaker in programs sponsored by such government agencies as the United State Office of Personnel Management; the Industrial College of the Armed Forces at Fort McNair, Washington, D.C.; the National Defense University at Indianapolis, Indiana; and the Marine Corps Training Center and Research Center at Quantico, Virginia.

Bob also became a participant in the programs of NYU's Faculty Research Network, whose mission was to address the needs of underserved colleges in the East, offering four-week summer institutes for their faculty. Between 1980 and 2010 Bob offered ten courses there and was the only participant who gave on-site seminars at Black colleges in the South, including Stillman College in Tuscaloosa, Alabama, and Tougaloo College in Tougaloo, Mississippi. He also spoke at Spellman College and Morehouse College in Atlanta.

In 1978 he was inducted into Adelphi University's Academy of Distinction, honoring his contributions to education. In 1987, 1989, and 1995, he was the recipient of the NYU College of Arts and Science Golden Dozen Award for teaching excellence. In 1990 he won NYU's Distinguished Teaching Medal.

He participated in extra-curricular activities, including a sixteen-year stint as a Faculty in Residence in a freshman dormitory housing over seven hundred students. He also served as the mentor to the Arts and Science Dean's Circle, composed of fifty of the most outstanding students at the college. During intersessions, he took the Circle on foreign trips, including visits to Egypt, China, Russia, Thailand, Greece, Turkey, Morocco, Brazil, Italy, and Germany. In addition, for twenty-five years he served as an assistant coach of the NYU baseball team.

In 2002 he moved to NYU's Liberal Studies Program, which emphasized the study of great books. Later he taught in NYU's Stern College of Business, participating in a program titled "Personal Responsibilities and Leadership." There in 2019 he gave his final presentation at NYU.

Today he is professor emeritus, residing in Brooklyn with his wife, Kathryn, a psychotherapist, and staying in close touch with his two children: Sarah, a graphic artist, and Keith, a versatile, award-winning jazz musician.

PART I

TRIBUTES

I

Advisee, Colleague, Friend

Steven M. Cahn

Steven M. Cahn, the editor of this volume, is Professor Emeritus of Philosophy at the City University of New York Graduate Center.

During my five decades in academia, I have known a few faculty members who offered a philosophy course that regularly attracted a huge number of registrants. In nearly every case, though, the subject had special appeal, for instance, death and dying, justice, or happiness. Had the same professors taught less immediately appealing topics such as logic, medieval philosophy, or pragmatism, the enrollment would have been far smaller. The exception to this generalization is Bob Gurland, whose classes, regardless of subject matter, invariably filled the largest lecture halls at NYU. As it happens, logic, medieval philosophy, and pragmatism were all in his vast repertoire, as was virtually every course in the philosophy curriculum. Indeed, whatever subject he announced, the class was immediately oversubscribed.

Some professors enhance their enrollment by appealing to students who have a particular background or interest. Not so, Bob Gurland. Regardless of gender, race, ethnicity, talent, or preparation, students flocked to his offerings, and he reciprocated their passion by knowing the name of everyone in every class and learning something about each. Whereas instructors in large courses routinely employ assistants, Bob almost never did and always personally graded with numerous detailed comments, every one of hundreds of papers, thereby enabling him to communicate individually with each of his students.

This personal touch was exemplified in a story told by a friend of his who brought guests to have dinner with Bob in Greenwich Village. They were to meet him at his office on the seventh floor of the building that housed the philosophy department. Beforehand, his friend assured the visitors that as they all walked to the restaurant, Bob would greet by name at least a dozen students. As his friend laughingly told me, that prediction was fulfilled before they even left the office building.

In light of the skepticism of some colleagues about the source of his popularity, Bob welcomed, even without prior notice, anyone who wished to observe his classes. He also allowed colleagues to review the exams he gave, the answer booklets his students submitted, and the grades he awarded (which were not especially generous). The vast majority of those who watched him teach or scrutinized the written record came away impressed.

Why was he so successful? Admittedly, Bob has a most engaging personality and a wonderful sense of humor that pokes fun equally at himself and others. He also draws on his singular background that includes stints as a baseball player for local club teams, a professional trumpeter in leading jazz bands, and extensive experience teaching mathematics and science in elementary school, junior high school, high school, and college. Above all, whereas most faculty focus on their subject and expect the students to recognize its importance, Bob focused on the students and sought to demonstrate why the subject should matter to them.

In class his approach might have appeared improvisatory, but when I once asked him how he prepared to teach, he opened his battered briefcase and held up stacks of yellow pads filled with writing. He explained that these were his lectures, and although he never looked at them during his classes, he knew exactly what material he was going to cover and how it would be presented. Even his vivid examples were written down. In short, his seemingly freewheeling style was usually carefully planned.

He won teaching awards at a variety of institutions, but such honors meant far less to him than the enthusiastic response of his students. They included many of the most accomplished undergraduates, a number of whom, influenced by him, became highly successful professors of philosophy. He gave guest lectures at West Point then taught there full-time for two years and was a hit with officers and cadets.

Although my initial relationship with Bob was as his dissertation advisor, we soon became colleagues, then dear friends, and over the years I have cherished the hours we have spent together. They always leave me with the same joy in life that he transmitted to his students.

Their enthusiasm once led to an unprecedented crisis. It occurred in the late 1960s, a time of disruption that frequently involved sit-ins. On one occasion a throng blocked the entrance to the Dean's office and demanded action to deal with an unjust policy of the school. What was the complaint? A course cap of 200 that prevented the protestors from enrolling in Professor Gurland's course.

Understandably, some professors were rather perturbed when they contrasted their small class sizes with his mammoth ones. Yet they recognized that without him registration in the department would have plummeted because he taught a massive percentage of all the students taking philosophy. Indeed, some of those who regularly registered for his courses joked that they majored in Gurland.

Unlike some in the department who sought to minimize or disparage his success, I found his extraordinary effect on students to be not merely impressive but exhilarating. Indeed, I consider myself fortunate to have witnessed the phenomenon.

I realize that some who did not know Bob will presume that I am exaggerating his impact. Those who sat in his classes, however, confirm my account and are eager to add their own memories of his magic.

2

On Inspiration

Joseph Di Salvo

Joseph Di Salvo is the founder and managing partner of the law firm Di Salvo Howard PLLC, and adjunct professor at NYU's Stern School of Business.

In the summer of 1990, I was seated in an NYU amphitheater-styled classroom between my mother and father at an event for prospective new students. I was a first-generation everything: first to be born in the United States; first to attend college; first in the family to look beyond the immediate confines of a small, insular Italian-American working-class community in Queens, New York. My hope was to discover the opportunities that life can offer through the experience of higher education.

But I was scared, surrounded by kids (and their folks) who appeared to be far more ready for college: polished, worldly, prepared, confident. I felt overwhelmed, intimidated by the thought of everything riding on my performance in fulfilling my immigrant parents' American dream. I wasn't sure I could cut it.

Then Professor Robert Gurland appeared on stage.

He was to deliver a lecture titled "Introduction to Philosophy." When he strutted to the podium, he did not look like what I expected a professor to look like. He wore a purple sweater, fitted black jeans, and a silver charm in the shape of a trumpet swinging from his neck. His thick head of hair was slicked back, like a 1950s Vegas crooner in his prime. He was compact and muscular, five-and-a-half-feet tops, equal parts Harvey Keitel and Dustin Hoffman.

"Philosophical inquiry into our experience of life is important and necessary," he began, in a thick New York accent, "because it can help us answer the deepest questions that challenge our modern world, such as: Why doesn't an oat bran muffin taste like chocolate? Seriously, why are almost all the best-tasting, most delightful treats in our lives somehow determined to be bad for us? And all that is good seems to require sacrifice or compromise or—worse—suffering. Where's the justice in that?"

He gave us all a moment to ponder.

"While we're on the subject of injustice, let me bring up something you're all thinking about right now: size. Don't let anyone tell you differently. Size matters! Take it from me—and Napoleon. We would've given anything to be even a little bit taller. I'm still hoping that short works out better for me, though. We'll see."

Somehow—and I don't know how—he seemed to be talking at once to everyone and to no one. "You're all sitting there wondering, when does the philosophy begin? How will I know it? Will a bell ring? Will I suddenly feel smarter? You'll know you're engaged in philosophy if the questions you're asking and the answers you're receiving are making you uncomfortable. For the next hour—for some of you, I hope, for the next four years—we're going to be challenging many of the things you take for granted, which means that many of the certainties and basic assumptions that define your perspective will be undermined. Are you ready? Does that sound more like a rollercoaster or a torture chamber?"

There was enthusiastic assent, from students and maybe even more from parents.

"Okay, and I know what many of you are thinking right now, too," he continued. "What could I possibly learn from Socrates, an old white guy who lived in 400 BC? I'll tell you what. Was

Socrates different from you? He woke up in the morning. He put his feet on the same ground that you do. He got out of bed. He had a wife. Her name was Xanthippe. Okay, maybe no one here is named Xanthippe. Maybe you don't know any Xanthippes. Is there a Xanthippe in the house? By the way, Socrates' Xanthippe was a nag. She would say, 'Socrates! Why don't you go out and make money like the Sophists do? We need new sandals!' And he did. He tried to support his family, like many of you will do someday. He had kids—ditto. He went to the market every day—the agora, the ancient Greeks called it. By the way, anyone here ever have an egg cream at Agora, the ice cream parlor on Eighty-Seventh and Third? Jesus, for those egg creams you'd think twice about selling your own mother . . . where was I?"

"Agora!" someone yelled out.

"Agora! Thank you! Yeah, Socrates had hopes and dreams and disappointments, just like you and me. His most famous student, Plato, once said, 'Be kind, for everyone you meet is fighting a harder battle.' I think it's fair to say that his words didn't just apply to ancient Athens. So Socrates was out there, just like you and me. He was having conversations with friends about whether to go to war with Persia or whomever. You want to know the real difference between you and Socrates? If he got hemorrhoids, he didn't have Preparation H!" Gurland didn't wait for the laugh to die. "So. you think it might be interesting to see how this guy dealt with life? And why he thought the way he did? And how that might be of use to you?"

For the next forty-five minutes, without benefit of notes, Gurland riffed on complex thoughts concerning logic, existential conflict, ethics, human nature. He wasn't lecturing us as much as challenging us to question our preconceptions. His words fired into the air in a staccato rhythm in a deep Bronx (I would learn) accent, as if he was propelling the ideas out through a horn. When he stopped pacing, his eyes were closed, immersed in the wake of his words as deeply as his audience, maybe more.

Plato. Aristotle. Nietzsche. Kierkegaard. Ronald Reagan's role as actor, politician, and pop-culture redeemer. *Saturday Night Live* as the voice of cultural dissent. Michael Jackson's creativity and tragic story: all over the place and yet everything connected. At one point, Gurland said, "It's hard to win an argument on earth if the principles you're arguing against are supernatural. There's never any agreement on the ground rules, and even if there is for a moment, the otherworldly side always seems to have room to shift." (This hit with particular force, given my strict Roman Catholic upbringing and my subsequent painful struggles with it.)

He talked about the eternal human need for hero worship, then the morality of euthanasia. He asked us, "How much of your freedom are you willing to trade for your security? How much of that trade is apparent to you?" He explored the cultural ethos that existentially predisposes New Yorkers to be either a Mets fan or a Yankees fan, never both. He opined, "It's not enough for you to ask what the rules are. I want you to ask why the rules are." It was enthralling and intoxicating, especially for a 17-year-old, and I felt as if I had never been more intellectually engaged my entire life. And technically, this wasn't even a real class!

If all that wasn't enough, he shifted from abstract questions and esoteric ideas about cultural and social landscapes to the point of it all: "Whether it's here at NYU or anywhere else, your ability to think about these things and use the answers you devise to make your life better, to create meaning from your experiences, and to provide a richness to your life intellectually, personally, morally—that opportunity is priceless." A pronounced, dramatic pause followed, as Gurland let the thought hang in the air, his eyes shut, a hand on his chin. Most of the parents were nodding, smiling, while the other teens stared at the prophet on stage. My mind was exploding with inspiration and an energy I had never before felt.

"Time is the currency of love," he went on. "It is the most valuable commodity you have. You don't know how much you'll be given or how much of it you'll be able to control; those with whom you share it and the objectives that you pursue with it will define the richness and sense of fulfillment in your life. The study of philosophy provides you with the framework to ensure that the expenditure of your time enables you to feel that sense of enlightenment that . . . from time to time," he paused and smiled again, "makes the whole ball of wax worthwhile."

And that was it. Date, hour, minute, second.

That was precisely the moment my adult journey began. NYU was my destiny.

Gurland wasn't done holding court, captivating and mesmerizing the audience, but me above all. Yeah, college students were a tough crowd, he said, but nothing like grade-school kids, to whom he had taught math at the start of his career. "Here, I pretend to know the answer—I do it most of the time, by the way—and no one will give me a hard time. Ten-year-olds? Are you kidding? They ask questions you'd better have an answer for, and a good one. And right away. A thousand years ago I was teaching math, not philosophy, and I had to get the kids to understand multiplying negative numbers and positive numbers, so I gave them the rule: A negative times a negative equals a positive. Just memorize it and you got it, right? No, not right. One girl raises her arm and says, 'Why?' 'Why?' I repeat back to her, the oldest trick in the politician's bag, repeat what they asked when you don't have a clue. 'Why is a negative times a negative a positive?' she says, though we both already knew that that's what she meant. 'Why?' I say again, a little slower to buy time, and now I have the whole class staring at me. 'Why?' And now I know they think something's wrong with me."

Gurland closed his eyes, remembering. "Then I say, 'Okay, well, let's see . . . a positive number times a positive number is positive because . . . when a good thing happens to a good person, it's good. A negative times a positive is negative because when a bad thing happens to a good person, that's bad. A positive times a negative is negative because when a good thing happens to a bad person, that's bad. And a negative times a negative is positive because when a bad thing happens to a bad person, that's good!'" He opened his eyes, triumphant. "And that, Q.E.D, *quod erat demonstrandum*, is how you get to be a philosophy teacher."

I don't know which predominated: gasps of recognition and appreciation, laughter, or applause. My mother nudged my arm. I looked at her, her eyes and smile equally wide. I could tell she was happy to see how enthralled I was by this powerful little man on stage. She leaned toward me. "You might never leave this place," she whispered.

My father saw the exchange and nudged me too. "I'm glad you're paying for half of this," he uttered, louder than a whisper, but with that ironic smile I'd inherited from him, love masquerading as sarcasm.

Yes, my adult journey had begun—officially, in my mind, if in no one else's. And at that moment I experienced two transformative realizations.

First: I *can* do this. Sitting there in the amphitheater, I could feel my confidence and courage as a college student growing. Here was this guy with a genuine, old-school, outer-borough accent, commanding the room in a way you'd dream about. He was the one the university had called on to close the deal with the accepted high school seniors and their parents. He was the rockstar attraction used to market the school and its offerings. I started to believe that it was possible for me to be like that and sound like that and build my own success while being unapologetic about where I was from and the journey that would bring me to key moments in my life. All my youthful insecurities began melting away.

Second: I *want* to do this. Lecturing college students, moving them, challenging them, inviting them into a world where the most meaningful, profound questions get asked and explored (and maybe, occasionally, even answered). Arming them to find their way through logic and reason to appreciate the significance of morality and empathy and humor. It was the first time I remembered thinking about a future goal that would continuously influence my ambitions, my plans, and what I wanted to achieve in my intellectual life. It was the first time I remember feeling inspired.

3

A True Blessing

Ann Conti

For almost twenty years, Ann Conti taught mathematics and science in high school and college. She is now a deacon in the Episcopal Church.

As a first-year student at NYU in the 1970s, we actually met with an advisor to register. I had declared my major as philosophy, and he asked me if I minded an early class. When I said "no," he said, "then I will put you in the class with our most popular professor." And the path opened.

How I loved you from minute one! Warm and funny, smart and energizing, oozing with love of teaching and empowering others. You gave us notes the very first day, as I have done with my students for all the classes I have taught.

On my first exam I got a B+. You added the remark "But I liked your paper anyway." And I believed you. I appreciated your distinguishing between my test score and your encouragement that my ideas and writing had value.

I took a class (sometimes two) with you every semester except the last because Advanced Placement credits had left me with a single required course to take, and I couldn't ask my parents to spend the extra money.

At the end of spring semester as a junior, I had an existential moment and decided to take a year off. By that time, I was a double major in mathematics and philosophy and needed a sign-off from both advisors. My math professor wouldn't sign until I spoke with a school psychologist. This took time. Once I was certified as not looney, he signed off on my big plan. I then went to you.

"Professor Gurland, will you sign this? I'm going to take a year off." You asked me why.

"Well," I explained, "I feel like I need a break, and maybe I'll do something different for a while." You asked to see my schedule.

"Nah, you don't want to stop now. You have just one year left to go. Get the degree," you instructed, half-parent, half-teacher. With a wake-up shake to my shoulders, you added, "Then do what you want. Drop Ancient Greek—your schedule is too heavy."

I should have gone to you first. That psychology interview was ponderous. So, I need to thank you for my first degree, which enabled my other two and the M.Div. I'm currently working on.

To this day I love philosophy for its search for truth and first causes. I carry the anecdote you told us about William James arguing for the need of all people to appreciate philosophy's importance. Using a landlord as an example of a common man, James explained that landlords who think they need to know how much money tenants have in the bank really need to know their renters' personal philosophy that will reveal if they'll use the money to pay the rent.

I always used the flaw in one of Descartes' proofs of God's existence (the idea of an infinite being does not have to be infinite) as a question for my math students. And it was so interesting to see the good math students look blank, while someone good in English or just logical gets it and, with it, a shot of confidence.

I haven't become famous, rich, or written a book. I don't have a following on YouTube or TikTok, but I have more than enough for comfortable living and six to ten students who keep in touch with me. My sermons are well liked for their clarity and relatability.

And the person I am was hugely influenced by what you taught me both in classes and by example.

I love you, Bob. Love that comes from true understanding and sharing and honesty and growth and joy and wisdom is the best because it never diminishes. It only gets deeper and wider and welcomes more people. That is what you have done, Bob, for so many.

4

Bringing Philosophy to Life

SUSAN BRAEUER DAM

Susan Braeuer Dam is the Director of Research and Publications at the Calder Foundation in New York.

YOU ONCE SAID THAT when we find our philosophy in life, the feeling is akin to waking up in the middle of the night in our childhood bedroom and being able to find our way to the bathroom in complete darkness without bumping into anything. Those weren't the exact words, of course—and without your scintillating delivery they fall flat on the page! But to this day they carry the same and immediate force in my mind as they did in the late 1990s, when I was a student of yours. And it was in your "American Philosophy" class that I found myself back in that childhood home, so to speak, with William James's *Pragmatism*.

As a student in the Gallatin School of Individualized Study, I didn't fully immerse myself in the Department of Philosophy. But I did enroll in as many of your classes as I could fit into my schedule, from "Introduction to Philosophy" to "American Philosophy" to "Philosophy and Literature." I also snuck into a few that were full. (A lot of us did!) And even though I was too shy to ever introduce myself to the Bronx Socrates, your lessons formed the basis of not only my final oral exam, the Colloquium, but also my career.

When I think of how I navigated the world post-graduation, I sometimes think of the popular adage "Chance favors the prepared mind." Thanks in large part to you, my mind was prepared to recognize where I, in my deepest sense, belonged: A few years after graduating, while working at a museum, I watched a mobile by Alexander Calder unfold unpredictably in space—a live experience, activated by the unseen caprices of nature—and I was struck by how philosophy, life, and art coalesced in moments. Not in a finite way, but in a merging, overlapping way, pulsating with energy and rhythm.

I understood immediately that Calder's mobiles resonated so deeply with me because they restored a continuity between art and life as described in Dewey's *Art as Experience*. (I wrote about that book in one of your classes and still remember how shocked I was at the volume of feedback in bright red ink!) What's more, I soon learned that Calder had been married to William James's great niece. Following an intuition set forth in your classroom, I switched gears and dedicated my career to preserving Calder's legacy under the guidance of the artist's grandson at the Calder Foundation in New York. I have been at the Foundation for seventeen years as Director of Research and Publications.

Thank you for meeting me where I was at—where the "souls" of my feet hit the pavement—with lessons that continue to reverberate in my life. Much like Dewey called for art to be removed from its remote pedestal, you removed philosophy from the confines of the university's walls and set it within the stream of our experience. As you enter your tenth decade, you also enter my fifth decade, and the decades of so many others of all ages who continue to share your brilliance with their friends, family members, students, and colleagues—uniting generations!

Calder engaged the fourth dimension of time in his mobiles, and "time," as you say, "is the currency of love." It is with tremendous gratitude that I look back on your role in guiding my trajectory through life's greatest currency, in dialogue with James, Dewey, and Calder.

5

An Indelible Impact

Mark Yokoyama

Mark K. Yokoyama received his BA degree from NYU as a member of the class of 2019.

I am writing to express my deepest gratitude for your profound impact on my life. With great pleasure and admiration, this letter acknowledges the importance of my experiences with you as a teacher and highlights your lasting influence on my career trajectory, professional life, successes, and perspectives.

First and foremost, I am grateful for the invaluable guidance and mentorship you provided during my studies at NYU. Your passion for philosophy and ability to convey complex ideas with clarity and enthusiasm was truly inspiring. Your thought-provoking lectures and engaging classroom discussions instilled in me a deep appreciation for critical thinking and the pursuit of knowledge. Your dedication to nurturing intellectual curiosity fostered an environment that encouraged me to explore new ideas, challenge my assumptions, and develop a more complete understanding of the world.

My investing career is one aspect of my life where your influence has been particularly significant. The analytical and logical reasoning abilities I honed under your guidance have proven indispensable in this field. Your emphasis on critical analysis and examining different perspectives has allowed me to approach investment decisions with a more comprehensive and nuanced understanding. Your teachings have given me a strong foundation in evaluating risk, making informed judgments, and adapting to a constantly evolving market. I credit my professional success to the principles and insights I acquired through your teachings.

Moreover, I am grateful for the personal growth I experienced due to your mentorship. Your lessons shaped my intellectual development and overall approach to life. Through your guidance, I learned the importance of resilience and adaptability. You helped me navigate the challenges of transitioning from a nuclear refugee in Japan to a typical expatriate in Hong Kong. You gave me the tools and perspectives to embrace new cultures and forge meaningful connections with individuals from diverse backgrounds.

Your mentorship has also profoundly impacted how I perceive and manage success. Rather than focusing solely on achievements, you encouraged me to view advancement as an ongoing process of personal growth and continuous learning. Your unwavering support and belief in my abilities gave me the confidence to take on new challenges and pursue ambitious goals.

As I reflect on the scope of your legacy, it becomes evident that your influence extends far beyond the classroom. Your experience as a teacher and mentor is singular. You have positively shaped the lives of countless students, empowering them to become lifelong learners and contributing members of society. Your passion for education and your unwavering commitment to your students serve as an inspiration to us all.

In conclusion, Professor Gurland, I want to express my heartfelt appreciation for your transformative impact on my intellectual journey, career, and individual growth. The lessons I learned under your tutelage continue to guide me in my professional and personal endeavors. Your dedication, wisdom, and passion for teaching have left an indelible mark on my life, and I am forever grateful for the privilege of being your student.

6

Happy Accident

ANNA HART

Anna Hart is a public school teacher in New York City.

I REGISTERED FOR ROBERT Gurland's class by accident. My counselor insisted that I had to complete one more liberal arts course. I argued that I had completed my core requirements in high school, but my counselor wouldn't budge. I was infuriated that I had to pay for another liberal arts class. What was worse was that the only class I could fit in my schedule was a philosophy class! I was a serious student and did not have time for these easy, first-year, liberal arts classes that I would never ever need in my life ever . . . or so I thought.

I was a diligent student. I took extensive notes. I did all my readings the night before class, and I had a list of questions pertaining to the subject matter every day. I was armed with my winning strategy of taking notes on everything the professor said because that's what would be on the exams. This strategy was working well for me. I had a 4.0 grade point average and was given no notes on my assignments.

Until Gurland.

If you have had the opportunity to experience a Gurland class, you would know that it is humanly impossible to take notes on everything he says. Believe me, I've tried. I was using one to two pages for lecture notes in all my other classes but in Gurland's class, I needed at least fourteen pages, both sides, and in the margins. One day in the middle of a lecture (as I was massaging my aching hand), I had a series of resentful thoughts: these notes are moving far afield from the assigned readings, so why am I taking them? This professor has no idea who he's even talking to as it was a large room with hundreds of students. And this professor seems to have his eyes closed! So, with the mounting pressure of in-class tests on the horizon, I determined that I would skip Gurland's class and use that time to study for my other classes.

And fate steps in.

For it was on the very day when I skipped Gurland's class for the first and only time in my life, the fire alarm was pulled. As everyone spilled out onto the street, Gurland was standing right in front of me and turned around and said, "Where were you this morning?" Seeing no graceful way out, I told him the truth. I explained that I had a lot of tests that day and I thought I could just catch up with his class later and use the extra time to study. Gurland then asked me if I did well on the tests. He didn't scold me. He didn't make me feel bad for skipping his class. He just wanted to know if it worked out well for me. He even offered to answer any questions I might have about the class during his office hours. What he didn't know was that I had a million questions about the hundreds of things he said in class and how they actually connected to the readings. What was I supposed to know about this stuff? And how did he even know that I was a student in his class?

Armed with a list of questions, I went to see Gurland at his office hours. When I arrived, twenty students were lined up waiting to talk to him. I was ready to leave when I thought: If all these people are here to talk to him, maybe he knows a lot. I should wait and talk with him.

While I waited, the students were talking effusively about how Gurland was the best professor at NYU. I was not convinced.

When I entered his office, I was struck by the fact that his philosophy office was decorated with jazz photos—different. I sat down and began to ask question number one.

As Gurland began answering my first question, I took notes and moved on to questions numbers 2 through 20. As he answered, I jotted down notes and repeatedly apologized for how many questions I had. Gurland assured me that there was absolutely no problem with the number of questions. I thanked him for his time, but as I was leaving I remembered another question, so I turned around and said, "Oh, one more thing." Gurland asked me if I was Columbo and if I was about to crack a case. I didn't feel like Columbo. I felt seen, heard, and capable. I don't know how Gurland did it, but he made me feel like I was an excellent student even though I had just skipped his class not four hours before.

At that time, I was dorming with a woman from Hong Kong who could barely speak English. Her name was Polly, and aside from niceties, I hadn't really talked to her even though we lived in the same room. But on that day, I was so inspired by Gurland's office hours that I told her everything that happened that day. She listened and nodded politely until she suddenly said, "Aye! Did he do the freshman orientation lecture?" I told her I didn't know. She explained that there was a "philosophy guy" that was so inspiring that she almost switched her major to philosophy. We sat up the rest of the night talking about this "philosophy guy." Polly described him as a small man wearing Big John Jeans and a polo shirt that didn't have a true Polo insignia. With Polly's detailed description, we figured out that my professor and her "philosophy guy" were one and the same. We have been best friends since that day. In fact, I am writing this piece from a hotel in Hong Kong, where I am visiting Polly right now.

I signed up for every class that Gurland taught, and if I couldn't take his class, I audited it. I would often call home and recite lectures to my mother so that she wouldn't miss any of it.

Everyone who knows me knows Gurland because I will invariably mention him. To say that he is my professor misses the profound effect that Gurland has had not only on my intellectual life but also on my actual life. Long before the educational buzzwords of "Social Emotional Learning" or "Trauma Informed Instruction," Gurland was there for all his students meeting them where they were, making them feel seen, and heard, and safe, and trusted, and capable.

In regular classes you are assigned a paper, and you get it back with a teaching assistant's grade written on it. In Gurland's class, your paper comes back annotated with extensive guiding notes from Gurland. Often these notes are extending your thoughts and inspiring you to dig deeper into your topic. But sometimes the notes are hard life lessons. I will always remember the Gurland paper that came back to me with many notes, including the final comment: "Your conclusion lacks rigor." LACKS RIGOR! The amazing trick about that note was it was exactly what I needed to learn, and to this day it continually inspires me to do my due diligence.

In logic class, I practiced the logical argumentation elements and over-studied for the final exam. Logical argumentation was a difficult subject, and I wanted to master it. One of the exam questions was to prove a statement to be either true or false. The statement was: if p then q, and if p then r, therefore, if not q, then not r. I ran the truth tables and came back with the statement is true. When I got the exam back, Gurland had written: "If you're in Brooklyn, then you're in NY; if you're in Brooklyn, then you're in the US; therefore, if you are not in NY then you are not in the US . . . What about Peoria?" That phrase is in my head every time I try to solve something. Just when I think I've worked it all out, I stop and think "What about Peoria?" just to make sure I really understand the solution.

To say Gurland was wise counsel to his students is not the whole truth. He has a magical way of being present and showing up for his students in ways that seem inexplicable.

Hurt by a seemingly personal attack from a professor, I began wandering the streets around the University when suddenly there was Gurland. He immediately asked, "What's wrong? You don't look happy." I explained that a professor had said something mean to me and that I was really sad about it. Gurland offered to beat the professor up which made me laugh. He then explained, in true Gurland fashion, "Look, kiddo, you're going to meet jackasses in your life. You can't fall apart when a jackass crosses your path." And just like that, I was fine with that mean professor.

After my first and most devastating heartbreak, Gurland was there on a bench in Washington Square Park, listening to my 20-year-old self recounting how I had messed up my whole life. I told Gurland that I felt so vulnerable, and everything was making me feel so weak. Gurland said, "Kiddo, vulnerability is just evidence that you have the capacity to be hurt, and unfortunately, life is full of hurt. It's how we grow . . . life also has good things too . . . like cannolis." This made me laugh, and in that moment, I knew I would be okay. He guided me through it with compassion and wisdom and humor in a way that no one else could.

After 9/11 when the whole city was uneasy, I was walking around the East Village literally contemplating whether a transplant like me should even live in New York. I had almost convinced myself that I should return to Canada. Walking around thinking it through, searching for the right answer, I looked up and there was Gurland, outside a firehouse reading a 9/11 memorial. Within a few minutes, Gurland had once again reassured me in a difficult time. I can't even remember what he said, but I remember walking away feeling secure in NYC again.

The truly magical part is that I am not the only person who has experienced these unbelievable moments. Gurland, like no other person I have ever known, manages to provide this inexplicable patient and persistent presence in both the mind and the body. And to think that if I had successfully argued my counselor out of registering me for that philosophy class, I could have missed it. In hindsight, I am so thankful that I had no logical argumentation abilities back then, for that lost argument, the best loss ever, gave me exactly what I needed, every day, always.

7

A Memorable Lesson

Brian Smyth

Brian Smyth owns a title insurance agency in New York.

I SPENT THREE MONTHS of my life with Bob Gurland as my teacher, and that has made all the difference in my life. To this day I speak of him to all my friends and family. I mimic his voice as I tell the tales. In my life everyone knows Bob, everyone loves him, and no one has even met him. He's that interesting person in everyone's life whose virtues we constantly extol, and stories about him always end with "But that doesn't do him justice; you have to meet him to understand."

Bob once told me that people die twice. The first time is when your heart stops beating; the second time is when your name crosses someone's lips for the last time. If this saying is true, Bob is going to outlive us all. We are never going to be like him, we are never going to have what he has, and we are never going to have as much of an effect per capita as he has. The great gift is that we all know him, were smart enough to stay in touch with him, and secretly and unknowingly agreed that what he was offering was different from what all others were offering. He gave us his full attention, remaining with us until we understood the answer. He gave us his advice, remaining honest even if telling us something we didn't want to hear. Most importantly, he gave us his time, something he refers to as "the currency of love," which is a beautiful way to look at something that is slowly killing us all.

Time is our most precious commodity; it is a non-renewable resource. We cannot make any more of it, and once it runs out, its absence is permanent. What greater gift can someone as intelligent and talented as Bob bestow upon the world than to spend the majority of his time, his life's currency, giving away all that he knows, educating us all in a way that made us realize that we really hadn't truly been educated before? What can be said of a person who could have attained success in many ways but for six decades chose to read and grade every single paper his students wrote? He could have used his obvious gifts to do well for himself but chose instead to do good for others.

Here is one story about him that I shall never forget. (Please understand that what follows is what I remember. What he actually said and how he said it surpass my ability to report.) The second work in our course in "Philosophy and Literature" was Patrick Suskind's *Perfume,* a novel about an outcast named Grenouille, who was born with an extraordinary sense of smell but without a human scent. He eventually becomes a murderous perfumer whose scents are so powerful that he uses them to control people's lives.

From the first day of Bob's class, the students stood in awe of him, so we had a tacit agreement that Bob would tell us what he knew, we would write it in our notebooks, and when the class ended, we would all be smarter than when it began. Unfortunately, one student was at times a terrible distraction, constantly needing to be heard. After a series of his continuing interruptions, our class began exhibiting its displeasure with eye rolls and audible exhalations of frustration. Had this situation continued, at best the value of the course would have been reduced and at worst ruined.

Bob, always humble, generous, and kind when dealing with his students, set out to mitigate the situation. When he entered the third or fourth day of class, he looked at us with a puckish grin and said "Hi, guys" in such a winsome way that you felt you were old friends. As he walked to his desk to drop off books and papers, we saw a hand go up and knew immediately which student had raised it. As Bob turned back toward the class, he said to that student, "Oh, hello there," spoken with such charm that the entire class, including the student, chuckled congenially. "Is this a question about *Perfume?*" "No," replied the student. Bob continued, "Okay, but before I answer your question, could I first have a word?"

Like everyone else, I didn't know what Bob meant. Was he asking this student to step out in the hallway? Was he planning to embarrass him? Everything I knew about Bob led me to believe he would do nothing of the sort. The student lowered his hand and asked, "A word?" Bob released all the tension by replying, "Yeah, just a word, whatever word pops into your head." As it turned out, Bob had no intention of admonishing this student but just wanted him to choose a word at random.

I don't know what word I would have chosen, but I probably would have looked around for something to fill the void. The student did likewise and, scanning the room quickly, he saw a school flag and chose to repeat the word emblazoned on it: "Violet," he said confidently. "Violet!" Bob shouted, "Good god, you couldn't have made this easier on me, kid! Where did you get violet from?" he asked jokingly, giving us the humorous reprieve to which we had become accustomed. He turned his head left and right comedically, eventually turning his entire body around to face the blackboard.

With his back toward us, he deliberately raised his arm, index finger extended. As we began to realize he had found the culprit our smiles turned to quiet laughter, whose level increased the closer he came to reaching his target. As he pointed to the purple and white NYU insignia emblazoned on the small flag with the word "Violets" written in script across the bottom, he turned his head but not his body, looking directly over his shoulder at the student and said "Gotcha!" With this we all let out a crescendo of laughter, having been in on the joke together.

His back still toward us and his face turned again toward the blackboard, he said, "You know, I don't think I've ever noticed before that the thing says violets. I'm always thinking about the class but rarely pay attention to the classroom. I'm like the guy who goes for a walk but doesn't enjoy the scenery. I should change that; it seems there's value in paying attention to the small things."

Then he began running his hand through his hair while looking down at the floor, a habit we would come to recognize as his precursor to thought, and turning around to face all of us he began repeating, "Violet, violet, violet, violet, violet, violet," in that way we all do when a few seconds are needed to collect our thoughts. "You really screwed me here, kid," he said in his charismatic way. "Okay, I'll give it a shot," he said gently, "but don't hold it against me if this doesn't work out, okay babe? You know violet is a curveball, I was hoping for something a little easier to hit, something in my strike zone if you know what I mean." I still remember this line, as it was one of the many baseball references that would fill the room with laughter over the course of the semester.

"Okay, kiddo, violet it is," he said in an acquiescent way. Bob turned to us and began: "The interesting thing about your compatriot's word choice as it relates to Suskind's *Perfume* is that violet is both a color and a flower, which means, unlike concepts like 'happiness' and 'love,' violet can be understood aesthetically. We see violet, we know violet; we smell violet, we know violet. No questions asked. Millions of years of evolution have made our species understand the world two ways, intellectually and aesthetically."

Having never heard this distinction before, I was eager to learn what he meant. "Violet is understood aesthetically through our senses of sight and smell. We can appreciate it and understand its beauty simply by gazing upon it or by smelling it. That is, when we see or smell it, we understand its beauty instinctively. We must use our senses; explaining violet with language is essentially meaningless," he said emphatically. Then came a line that showed me how his mind works in very interesting ways: "Violet is a spiral staircase, not a door, it's easier to point to than it is to describe." I remember this particular statement because it was so simple and effective. I still use it to this day. Looking around the room he said, "Violet is not an abstract concept, people! It just exists, and always has. You don't need to intellectualize it as you would "honor" or "democracy." Violet is pre-consciousness. Violet is primal. Violet is primordial. It was there during the soup, during the ooze!" He said this in such a way that it made you think it was something he was realizing at the same time he was saying it. It was as if he was thinking: "Good thought, Bob," and although he was making it up as he went, he could now see the outline of the direction he wanted to take us.

"Smells, colors, sounds, and tastes came way before language, way before consciousness, which means they cannot be superannuated. Violet isn't going anywhere, babe, it was here before us, and it'll be here after us. You get it?" he asked all of us in a way that made it clear the ideas that followed were going to be contingent upon our understanding this concept as we were taken on this journey.

Pointing to the student who chose this word, Bob said in his charming, almost impish way, "This word is great, babe. It's a great word because it gets right to the heart of Grenouille's dilemma, which is this: What is the fate of a man who cannot be understood aesthetically? What is the fate of a man who wants to be violet, but cannot?" I didn't understand what he meant. None of us did, but he intuited this and helped us along by saying, "This Grenouille fella, he can create all the fragrances in the world. His sense of smell is so refined that he can break things down to their constituent parts in the correct amounts and rebuild them from memory when he needs to, but the poor fellow has no human scent. You can't smell the guy!" he said in very down- to-earth language. "So, unlike a violet, he can't be understood aesthetically. He's not violet because we cannot understand him through our senses, through our sense of smell." Moving on, Bob said, "The perfumes Grenouille creates can be known through our senses, but Grenouille himself cannot. He can recreate any scent in the world. His schnoz is so powerful Suskind tells us he could 'smell a worm in the apple,' but the one thing he will never be able to smell is himself."

"What is the meaning of this philosophically?" Bob thought for a second and then said, "Well, if we want to understand

Grenouille, Suskind tells us we need to use our nose, not our brain." Bob explained that "Grenouille lacks the olfactory sense that we as humans accept and in whose absence we inherently reject. From an olfactory and chromatic perspective, we could say that his existence is one that we can see but can never fully understand as one understands the scent of a violet."

Knowing what I know now, it's amazing that Bob had already established the connection he would eventually make. It's like reading a great mystery novel a second time where all the most important clues, hidden upon first read, become glaringly obvious upon our second. We always wonder how we didn't see it coming. Bob ended by saying, "I can make the argument that Grenouille wants to be understood in a way that is almost identical to the way violet is understood." Saying this seemed a mistake to me, as he was now going to have to create what I assumed would be loose metaphors to make a connection that never existed to begin with. I thought he was going to offer a watered-down version of whatever he had prepared to teach that day,

But then Bob began another approach: "I know a few things about violet, guys, and maybe you people would like to know them, too. I have no idea, maybe you don't," he said comedically, "but I'm going to tell you whether you want it or not because I'm the guy standing at the front of the room!" It was great stuff. He just had a way about him that made you understand that we were all in this thing together, even when he joked about our separation.

He paced a little bit and then said, "What's interesting about violet is that it's complex; it has an interesting history. Linguistically, colors like violet were introduced to languages in the late stages of their development. Simple colors and simple words are found in earlier stages, which makes sense: black and white, for example. Colors like reds, greens, yellows, and blues come a bit later, and eventually we start reading about pinks and violets. This is the normal trajectory for romance languages, English included." He continued, "So you know, we can see that in a strange way, violet is a smart color so to speak. Alright maybe it's not smart," he said jokingly. "But just go with it, you get my drift, don't look too deeply into it," he said in a self-effacing way. "Look if it ain't smart, it's at least more interesting than white," he said with a smile. "It's more complex because you need to combine two colors to make it. It's not primary, it's secondary." He then paused for a moment to see if we were all still with him, saying, "If you're represented by a color, be a complex color. Try not to have a black and white personality."

Then he took a new approach: "A lot of people think Shakespeare invented the word. That hack gets credit for everything," he said tongue-in-cheek. "It's in his sonnets, it's in *Hamlet,* it's in *Henry IV*, it's everywhere in his stuff. He loved violets, so they're all over these poems and plays. Violets are everywhere in Hamlet. Hamlet gives Ophelia violets when her father dies, and so on. But Shakespeare didn't introduce violet to us; he only helped popularize it. He mentioned violet and purple, which are the same thing, often enough that the groundlings began using the word, and over the course of time it became part of the English lexicon."

His knowledge stunned us, and then he continued, "But before Shakespeare was aware of the word 'violet,' it came from the ancient Greeks. In Tyre, for example, Tyrion purple was a dark violet colored dye used for the clothing of wealthy families. In Greek literature, purple is mentioned in both the *Iliad* and the *Odyssey*, a thousand years before Shakespeare. Eventually violet came to England and France, no longer as a dye but as a fully established royal color."

"So violet acts as a perfect metaphor for what Grenouille is versus what he wishes to become. Grenouille doesn't want to be understood intellectually. He wants to be understood aesthetically, as one understands the perfumes he creates. He doesn't want to be thought about in the minds of the Parisians. He wants to be smelled by them, but he cannot. So, unable to be understood aesthetically, he must gain acceptance through surrogate human scents. But this is nothing more than power. It is control. And power is best represented by violet."

It was such an interesting way to get to this single idea that I assumed this insight was the end of his lesson. What I didn't know at the time, what none of us could have known at the time, was the length of the bridge this lecture was going to span.

He went on: "Ladies and gentlemen, to this day the imperial state crown worn atop the head of the King of England is violet, as are the royal robes. Louis XV, the king of France at the time this novel takes place, wore the Cote-de-Bretagne in his crown, the largest and most important of France's crown jewels," Then asking in a waggish way: "Guess what color it is!" He paused for a few seconds, only to then remember something else, he shouted, "Even the French flag, the tricolore, has two primary colors, red and blue, which when combined make, you guessed it baby, violet! Grenouille would have known this!" he stated resolutely, only to then jokingly and self-deprecatingly state, "Maybe he wouldn't know this. Probably not. What do I know?" Quickly continuing this thought, he said, "What I am sure about is that violet has more to do with Grenouille than we think, and Suskind wants us to know this as well."

Not understanding what he meant, I dug deeper into my seat, waiting to see where he was taking this. "So by the eighteenth century," he continued his history lesson, "the period of this novel, we find violet universally understood in language and inextricably associated with royalty and power. In the same way we see violet sewn into the fabric of authority and sovereignty, draped over the shoulders of kings and queens. So, too, we find Grenouille desiring a type of royal power. Because he is unable to be understood through the senses, as a violet is understood, he is now manufacturing scents through the pressing of flowers, perhaps even violets," he said questioningly as he scanned the classroom for affirmation that it was an interesting point. He continued, "His combining of scents, his enfleurage, reduced or enhanced in greater or lesser amounts, is his attempt to be recognized aesthetically, his attempt to capture the intrinsic beauty of colors and flowers, his attempt to be understood as a violet is understood. But try as he might to be understood aesthetically, he cannot create his own scent. Why not? Because his scent isn't there to be smelled, so it isn't there to be created."

I had never learned so much about something so seemingly innocuous as how a color or a smell could represent the dynamism of a literary character. I had taken this possibility for granted, as we all had.

Never before had I heard anyone express such interesting historical and poetic details about something so seemingly simple. It was as if an entire world was opening to us. Unsure if I was alone in my amazement, I looked at the girl sitting next to me, and as she felt my stare, she turned to me, her face revealing a smile of disbelief. We both gave that universal head shake that asks the question, "Are you experiencing this the same way I am?" She was, we all were. It was awesome.

He said thoughtfully, "There is something in a violet that wants to be recognized! There is something in the immediate recognition of violet in this novel that makes it somehow more special than other colors and other smells. But what in this novel specifically brings us back to Grenouille?" He allowed us to sit silently for what seemed like eternity. Nobody knew the answer.

Putting us out of our misery he said, "When Grenouille left society and lived in a cave, Suskind tells us he created an imaginary world, which he refers to as his 'inner palace.' In this palace, Grenouille begins to amass and catalogue all the fragrances of the world, using them to create unlimited perfumes with endless variations and power. Is it not meaningful that he does this in a palace?" We all agreed. He then asked, "Is a palace not a home for a king? Do you not find it strange that in this imaginary perfumery Suskind tells us that Grenouille begins to refer to himself as 'Grenouille the Great'? He tells us that he has servants and maids, a further allusion to his perceived royal sovereignty."

The deeper the connections he made, the more incredible the lecture seemed. It didn't seem possible that he could create something like this out of nothing. But what followed was the magic trick he had been setting up since he heard the word "violet." He looked at us and asked, "In this imaginary world, what color does Grenouille paint the great room in which he stores his beloved scents? Suskind tells us it was purple. What color is the sofa that

Grenoille sits upon as he gazes upon his creation? Suskind tells us it was purple. What color is the perfume the Marquis fans Grenouille with? Suskind tells us it was pressed with violets. Most importantly, and perhaps most tellingly, what specific color is the color of Grenouille's heart?" We all immediately became aware that the answer was again and again violet.

It was astonishing. It was a simple literary detail that every single one of us had overlooked because we had assumed the color was chosen at random by Suskind the same way it was chosen at random by our classmate. Bob's immediate recognition of this small oversight on our part and his ability to reveal to us the overall importance of the color as it related to our protagonist was astounding.

A palpable chill of disbelief and recognition went through my entire body upon his pulling off this intellectual feat, and as my hair stood on end, I looked around the classroom: a hundred or so other students were having the same realization at the same time. We were having a peak experience without having to climb a mountain or run a marathon. It made you want to stand up and applaud, but as this was a classroom, that behavior seemed out of place.

In ten minutes, maybe less, Bob Gurland had taken us on a philosophical, historical, and literary journey through a single word chosen by a student at random. He had no way of knowing what word would be chosen; it could have been any word in the English language. The most amazing part was that the word didn't matter. Had it been another random word, he would have simply pivoted and found the connections to the text. Nothing was isolated. Nothing existed in a vacuum. All things were connected.

He ended this lesson by explaining, "Suskind made sure all these things were purple or violet, and I'll tell you why. Unfortunately for Grenouille his power is only represented by purple. It is not derived from it. Painting our houses purple does not make us royalty, and a king's power exists even when the robe comes off. In Grenouille's attempts to achieve complete authority over humanity, he fails to gain aesthetic acceptance because he will never be part of the prism through which we instinctively understand purple, through which we can smell a violet. He is not a recognizable human in the same way violet is a recognizable color. We cannot see him because we cannot smell him." The insight was mesmerizing.

He finished by telling us, "Sunsets are never described as imbued with hints, splashes, and undertones of authority. These descriptions are reserved for, and the sole province of, colors and smells, like violets or things created by evolution, not by man. His chosen color is violet, but his existence always remains outside the immediacy of our senses. Grenouille will never exist as other humans do. He can never be violet; he can only pretend to be. He can only fantasize about being understood this way. He lacks that primordial essence, that thing that has always existed, so he can never know what it means to be truly human. Violet is by nature aesthetic, and in this novel, the appreciation is always for the perfume, not for the scentless Grenouille."

Bob concluded with this final thought: "It's amazing when we consider how often fiction and reality intersect. Sometimes it seems like one is telling the other one's story. I just haven't figured out which direction it goes."

He then turned to the student who had raised his hand just minutes earlier and said with sincerity, "That turned out to be a great word, babe. You made me look great with that one," to which we all were able to finally release our withheld joy in one collective laugh. Then Bob said to him, "Okay, I apologize for making you wait. What's your question?" to which the student responded, "It's okay, you answered it."

As usual, the person Bob needed to rein in never felt in any way diminished. Quite the opposite, he came out with his ego fully intact, believing he was not a drag but the impetus for a successful class. Thus did Bob simultaneously bewitch and interdict.

The student was correct, though. Whatever his question was, even if it had nothing to do with Suskind's novel, it had been answered. There was no time to waste in this man's classroom; the lessons were going to be far too important. All our questions, whether we asked them or not, were going to be answered. All we had to do was listen.

8

Changing West Point

PETER STROMBERG

Brigadier General Peter Stromberg, U.S. Army, Retired, was Professor of English and Chair of the Department at the United States Military Academy at West Point.

YOU, BOB GURLAND, CHANGED West Point. You changed the composition of the faculty. You changed the required curriculum.

The notion of changing West Point was not on your mind when you persuaded NYU to allow you to accept the invitation to serve as Visiting Professor in West Point's Department of English during the 1976–77 academic year. You were probably attracted by the prospect of a radical, though potentially fascinating, change in your own environment. You knew that West Point was not NYU by a long shot. You may have hoped that the obvious order of the Academy would reinforce your own dedication to order. Perhaps you were intrigued by an invitation from such an unlikely institution and were curious about an English Department tinkering with philosophy. Or maybe the prospect of grueling drives between Northport and West Point in your battered pickup captured your imagination. Whatever your motives, they almost had to be essentially instinctive and refreshingly artless.

You were responding to the Academy's explicit desire for you to shine your star on cadets enrolled in an English course that they were all required to take in their last year of study. The course curriculum had for many years included both literary and philosophical texts even though no one on the faculty had academic credentials in philosophy. You were invited to invigorate and dignify the presentation of the philosophy element of the course. Despite West Point's long-standing commitment to small, discussion-oriented classes, it sought your colorful talent and your lauded skill in the lecture hall. It wanted a philosopher who loved to teach, a philosopher whose students loved him. The English Department wanted to capitalize on your knowledge and energy, your honesty and humor, if not your mastery of the flugelhorn.

The faculty of that department consisted of Army officers with graduate education in literature. They had distinguished themselves as officers leading troops in the field and had excelled as students in demanding graduate programs at some of the nation's best universities. MA degrees in hand, they were assigned to teach for three years at the Academy before returning to the field. They were fiercely dedicated to their students. Faculty members had a huge stake in the success of their students who would soon join them as serving officers in the field. Cadets themselves knew their teachers as outstanding officers who cared deeply about the academic discipline that they professed and about the development of future officers.

Because the senior-level English course included texts in philosophy as well as literature, the faculty members were eager for live support. You furnished that support and, of course, electrified cadets in the lecture hall with enrapturing raps on matters philosophical. And in the classroom, though lecturing on a smaller stage, you attracted many of the Academy's brightest students to your elective courses, particularly "Practical Reasoning," even though your courses did not fulfill a demand of their academic concentration. Those cadets overloaded for you.

You quickly became acquainted with the weird complexity of West Point. It had no academic majors, only "areas of concentration." Elective courses themselves, the first few having been cautiously introduced only sixteen years earlier, were outliers to core courses that had exclusively composed West Point curricula since 1802. The English Department itself taught four of those core courses. The Department of Electrical Engineering also taught core courses, the consequences of which were an unanticipated feature of your visit to the Academy.

The arrangements for your visit were completed at the beginning of the 1976 spring semester, a semester that ended horribly when the Electrical Engineering faculty discovered that scores of junior-year cadets enrolled in a core electrical engineering course had submitted homework that they appeared to have falsely represented as their own. If that was the case, they and any other cadets who were aware of their deception had violated the Academy's vaunted Honor Code. The discovery was devastating. In the summer of 1976, boards of officers questioned the suspects (supported by lawyers) to sort the copiers from those copied and to identify the cadets who knew but remained silent about a deception. Those boards determined that 153 cadets had violated the Honor Code; they either resigned or were separated. (Many members of that group applied for readmission, and exemplary post-Academy activities qualified a large portion of them to join the class of 1978.)

The Class of 1977 was decimated. The Academy lost confidence in its traditional reliance on the Honor Code to enable the faculty to treat homework as, in effect, an in-class examination. The Honor Code itself seemed to be on shaky ground. You arrived in late August at an institution in crisis. You also arrived with the first women ever to enter the Academy. Change was in the air. But no one expected you, the non-stop talker from the Bronx via NYU, to be an historic agent of change.

From the beginning, however, you embodied change by simply dressing as yourself. Although the Academy in the late sixties had hired a woman in civilian clothing to perform duties that included the teaching of an elective course on art history for the English Department, her few years in the classroom did not set a precedent. Leaders at the Academy continued to believe that civilian faculty members would somehow undermine the preparation of cadets for military service. The faculty remained uniformed (even the handful of civilian native speakers in the Department of Foreign Languages taught in a uniform). You were the school's first conventional Visiting Professor, conventionally attired like a preppy prof at a conventional university.

But lo and behold, the Academy did not crumble. Your dedication to teaching bonded you to a military faculty likewise dedicated to teaching. Your genius as a teacher bonded you to cadets who delighted in being taught well. You befriended multitudes beyond the English Department. When it sought approval to retain you as a Visiting Professor for a second year, the Dean and the Academic Board enthusiastically granted the request.

During the next dozen years, every other department followed suit and engaged civilian professors for yearly visits. By the nineties, West Point was hiring civilians for extended faculty service. Today about one-fifth of the Military Academy's faculty is routinely composed of contracted civilian academics. You broke the barrier. Your performance in your first year as Visiting Professor initiated a major change in the composition of the West Point faculty.

You stayed a second year despite pressures to return to the NYU fold and keep its Philosophy Department solvent. While most of your NYU colleagues sought academic success as far from the classroom as possible, you lived in the lecture hall teaching legions of students. You were the department's bottom line. It grudgingly yielded, nonetheless, to the argument that you would be helping a national institution steady itself. And you somehow convinced your wife and children on Long Island of the truth that your work at West Point was a patriotic necessity. It was not as though you were trading the weekday comforts of home for luxurious living at West Point. Your apartment in the Bachelor Officers Quarters was famously either undercooled or overheated. You had good friends on the Hudson but not a home. The distance between Northport and West Point remained the same. Your willingness to stay a second year was a noble sacrifice.

In your second year, 1977–78, you changed the curriculum. The possibility for change grew out of two actions. A commission formed by the Secretary of the Army and headed by Frank Borman examined the Honor Code and its impact on the Academy. The final report of the Borman Commission in late 1976 called for extensive changes at West Point. In the spring of 1977, a newly formed West Point Study Group grappled with the implications of the Borman report and recommended 152 specific changes. Among them was task number sixty-three to "institute a course in philosophy and ethics for Fourth Class or Third Class year." The course was to stress ethics, not in a naive hope that it would necessarily affect behavior but in the belief that it would provoke seriously informed thinking. The West Point Study Group and the Academy leadership agreed that such a course would greatly strengthen the required curriculum and might help cadets think more clearly about their principles and actions as cadets and as Army officers.

In the summer of 1977, Andrew Goodpasture, the retired NATO commander, was recalled to active duty as the new Superintendent of the Military Academy and was charged with implementing the 152 recommendations. He was particularly keen to create an environment that would sharpen the moral awareness of cadets, and you were prominent in his many conclaves. He pinned much of his hope on the successful implementation of the sixty-third recommendation and assigned responsibility for number sixty-three to the Department of English.

To fulfill its responsibility, the department needed expert help. First, it needed someone to identify the graduate philosophy programs appropriate for the Army officers who were then being selected for two years of study before they would join the faculty in the fall of 1980. Second, it needed someone to create the curriculum for the new sophomore-level course and select its supporting texts. Third, it needed someone to prepare members of the literature faculty to teach the new course that would begin in the fall of 1978. Because the Dean had endorsed the department's wish to move swiftly and efficiently, the number of faculty members to be prepared was substantial. The plan called for the replacement of the mandatory course for seniors with the new philosophy course. Because that course would be required for juniors in their senior year, the plan mandated that they join the seniors and sophomores as students in the 1978–79 philosophy course. The plan thus required that twenty-five literature teachers had to be prepared to teach philosophy to roughly 1,500 cadets in each of the two semesters.

You answered all three needs: the first and second inconspicuously, the third spectacularly. For four weeks following the end of the spring 1978 semester, you taught the new forty-lesson course that you had designed. You taught two lessons each day to those twenty-five officers. You showed the fledglings what they might do with each assignment. You answered their questions. You gave them knowledge they needed. They knew that they would not equal you, but their confidence in you strengthened their resolve to follow you.

And then you went away. NYU and your family were calling. You answered those calls, but not before you were tempted with the possibility of staying permanently at the Military Academy. The Dean was ready to push all the bureaucratic buttons necessary to make the Academy's prized visitor a resident faculty member, thus accelerating the change you had earlier put in motion.

Still, you went away. But your legacy persists. The Academy faculty prospers with civilian professors. The Department of English, which eventually became the Department of English and Philosophy, nurtured its philosophers so successfully for forty-six years that the philosophy program became a prized possession, thus purloined in the summer of 2024 by a Law Department eager for intellectual distinction and a new title, namely, the Department of Law and Philosophy. You, Bob Gurland, changed West Point.

Please, my dear friend, treasure that truth and the gratitude of all Americans who care about the moral strength of the nation, the Army, and the Military Academy.

PART II

ESSAYS

9

The Good Teacher

Sidney Hook

Sidney Hook, one of the twentieth century's leading social thinkers and longtime head of the Department of Philosophy at NYU, greatly admired Bob Gurland's teaching, describing it in a letter of reference as "phenomenal." This essay provides an account by Hook of the attributes of a good teacher that he later found exemplified in Bob Gurland. Hook's reflections are drawn with omissions and minor stylistic changes from the last chapter of his classic work in the philosophy of education titled Education for Modern Man, *originally published in 1946, revised in 1963, and reprinted in 2020 by Wipf and Stock Publishers.*

What makes a good teacher, like what makes a good education, must be considered in relation to certain values. What we are seeking are the criteria of a good teacher in a democratic society.

(a) The first criterion is intellectual competence. By this I mean not only the truism that teachers should have a mastery of the subject matter they are teaching and that they should keep abreast of important developments in their field but that they should have some capacity for analysis. Without this capacity, they cannot develop it in their students.

Related to intellectual competence is the willingness to countenance, if not to encourage, rational opposition and spirited critical dissent by students. The inquiring mind even among youth sometimes probes deeply. Only teachers unsure of themselves will resent embarrassing questions to which the only honest reply must be a confession of ignorance. Intellectual independence is such a rare virtue that the good teacher positively welcomes it, despite the occasional excesses of youthful dogmatism and exuberance.

(b) Intellectual competence is necessary but not sufficient for good teaching. It must be accompanied by a quality of patience towards beginners which accepts as natural the first groping steps towards understanding by the uninitiated. The "simple" and the "obvious" are relative to antecedent skills and knowledge. Failure to see and act on this is responsible for intellectual brow-beating by otherwise competent teachers and for the air, deliberately only half-concealed, of suffering the hopeless stupidity of those who are stumbling their way forward.

The intellectually quick, and all teachers should be quick, have a tendency towards intellectual impatience. The impatience but not the quickness must be curbed. Patience is something that can be learned, except by certain temperaments who should never be entrusted with a class. Good teaching is not found where a star teacher holds forth for the benefit only of star pupils, but where some participating response is evoked from every normal member of the class. Nothing is easier than to yield to the pleasures of colloquy with the exceptional students of a class— and nothing is more unfair to the rest, in whom this builds up intense resentment, oddly enough not against the teacher but against their exceptional classmates. Special provision should be made for the instruction of superior students, but a good teacher does not let their special needs dominate the class to the exclusion of the legitimate educational needs of the others.

(c) The third characteristic of good teaching is ability to plan a lesson, without mechanically imposing it on the class, in those subjects where basic materials have to be acquired, and to guide the development of discussion to a cumulative result in subjects in which the seminar method is used. The bane of much college teaching is improvisation. Improvisation is not only legitimate but unavoidable in motivating interest and finding points of departure or illustration for principles. But it cannot replace the planful survey of subject matter and problems, nor provide direction to discussion. It is delightful to follow the argument wherever it leads. But it must be an argument. And it should lead somewhere.

What the teacher must aim at is to make each class hour an integrated experience with an aesthetic, if possible a dramatic, unity of its own. Without a spontaneity that can point up the give and take of discussion, and a skill in weaving together what the students themselves contribute, preparation will not save the hour from dullness. The pall of dullness which hangs over the memories of school days in the minds of many unfortunately envelops the whole question of education.

(d) Another important quality good teachers possess is knowledge of human beings. They are in a sense practical psychologists. They know something more than the laws of learning curves, and what they know they have not found in textbooks on psychology. The more one studies students, the more differences they reveal. These differences need not be relevant to what they are trying to learn, but sometimes they are. A teacher devoid of this knowledge cannot solve the problem of motivation or evoke full participation from the class. Nor can they tell when to temper the wind, when to let it blow, when to build up self-assurance in the pathologically shy, when to deflate the bumptious. Unable to diversify challenges, they cannot teach with proper justice and discipline in a class of miscellaneous talents. They may have a standard for the group; they should have a standard for each individual in terms of special needs—whether they be disabilities or advantages.

The secret of intellectual vitality in the classroom, when a theorem is being derived for the twentieth time or when an elementary point in the grammar of a foreign language is being explained or when the nerve of an old philosophic argument is being laid bare, lies in experiencing the situation as a fresh problem in communication rather than one in personal discovery. Or, putting it a little differently, it consists in getting the students to reach the familiar conclusion with a sense of having made their own discovery. The task is to make as many as possible see as much as possible of what they have not seen before. It is this perennial challenge, which cannot be adequately met without a knowledge of people, that keeps good teachers alive. If they do not recognize it, they are pedagogical automata, and almost always a bore.

(e) Good teaching requires sympathy, a positive attitude of imaginative concern with the personal needs of others. Those who teach large numbers and never get to know their students have a tendency to regard all but a brilliant few as a dull, cloddish mass. Reduce the number in each class, shorten the perspective, and no one worthy of being a teacher will fail to see the interesting variety of potentiality in every group. In each person there is some unique quality of charm, intelligence, or character, some promise and mystery that invites attention and nurture. The teacher who seeks it will find it.

Students respond to sympathy for their special intellectual needs like plants to sunshine and rain. They undertake more and achieve more. The function of the teacher is unobtrusively to raise the stick of achievement higher and to offer criticism without killing self-confidence. Students rarely disappoint teachers who assure them in advance that they are doomed to failure. They do not, of course, always live up to the more optimistic expectations of their teachers, but they invariably do the better for it.

Teachers must be friendly without becoming a friend, although they may pave the way for later friendship, for friendship is a mark of preference and expresses itself in indulgence, favors, and distinctions that unconsciously find an invidious form. There is a certain distance between teacher and student, compatible with sympathy, which should not be broken down —for the sake of the student. Teachers who court popularity, who build up personal loyalties in exchange for indulgent treatment, have missed their vocation. They should leave the classroom for professional politics.

(f) The good teacher, to close our inventory of traits, possesses vision. It is the source of both intellectual enthusiasm and detachment in the face of inevitable failures and disappointments. Without vision teachers cannot inspire a passion for excellence. The vision must not obtrude itself into the details of instruction. Its presence should be inferable from the spirit with which the instruction is carried on. It should operate in such a way as to lift up the students' hearts and minds beyond matters of immediate concern and enable them to see the importance of a point of view. Wherever an intellectually stimulating teacher is found, there will also be found some large perspective of interest that lights up the corners of subject matter. If students catch fire from it, it should not be in order to believe some dogma but to strengthen them in the search for truth and to become more sensitive to visions that express other centers of experience.

Teachers tend to take themselves too seriously and to regard the world as a classroom waiting for the proper lessons to solve the problems of adult experience. A sense of humor about themselves is the best assurance of a sense of proportion in these matters—a safeguard against taking themselves too seriously as well as against vain regrets.

It is not the emoluments and social status or holiday words of community praise which are criteria of success for teachers. Rather it is a twofold satisfaction. First, they are aware of being part of a continuing tradition which, no matter how humble their role in it, connects the great minds of the past with those of the present and future. Second, although teachers like actors are sculptors in snow and can leave no permanent monument of their genius behind, they can reach the minds of those who will survive, and through them affect the future. The lives of most people would have been pretty much the same no matter who their teachers were. But there are a sufficient number of men and women in the world who can truthfully testify to the determining and redetermining role which some teachers played in their lives. To very few is it given to exercise this influence. The opportunity to do so is a measure of both the power of teachers and their responsibility.

10

A Professor's Duties

PETER MARKIE

Peter Markie is Curators' Distinguished Teaching Professor of Philosophy Emeritus at the University of Missouri, Columbia.

BOB: FOR OVER FORTY years my memories of your teaching informed and sustained my own efforts. When my focus dimmed or enthusiasm lagged, I returned for guidance and inspiration to your essay "Teaching Mathematics" (an edited excerpt is reprinted in Chapter 13 as "The Challenge of College Teaching" —S.M.C.) Whenever I reread Sidney Hook's "The Good Teacher," you immediately came to mind. Here I want to reflect on the important lesson I learned from you and consider why it is easy to overlook and hard to follow.

We don't just teach a subject; we teach people. It's a lesson with multiple levels. As you've pointed out, our teaching needs to start where our students are: "To ignore the recipient [in the educational process] in favor of dedication to a subject creates the deadly environment that prevails in so many college classrooms today." The proper design of our courses should not be determined by our current research interests, favorite works, or the amount of time we wish to devote to grading, but by the needs and abilities of our students.

I first recognized this essential point when, fresh from your introduction to philosophy, I watched a friend slog through another professor's introductory course entirely devoted to skepticism, the subject of the professor's scholarship. The professor ignored the need to engage the concerns of his students. My friend responded the way you would expect, like someone who signed up for an introduction to Mediterranean cuisine only to spend the entire semester studying olives.

You taught me that good teaching demands not only a sense of the concerns and skills of our students but also a sense of them as individuals for whom we care. In "The Good Teacher," Hook characterizes such care as a form of sympathy, "a positive attitude of imaginative concern with the personal needs of others," and he notes that students "respond to sympathy for their special intellectual needs like plants to sunshine and rain. They undertake more and achieve more." Aware that your teaching had this effect on me, I strove to model it as I taught others. On more than one occasion when my interest in students waned, I reminded myself of the attention you gave me, the difference it made in my education, and the opportunity I had to offer it to others.

That our students are persons requires that we recognize and promote their autonomy. We are concerned with their intellectual and emotional development as human beings, with their acquiring the skills and habits for independent, critical thinking.

To teach in this way is to hope that students will change how they think. Teaching is thus subversive. We challenge and at times undermine students' conceptions of the world and themselves. We communicate the values and attitudes necessary for the rational search for truth: self-reliance, curiosity, a willingness to follow arguments and evidence wherever they lead, and a sense of the human condition that supports virtuous action. Teaching in this way is the opposite of the indoctrination that some higher education critics find behind every syllabus they examine. If we do our job properly, our students will travel by their own lights on rational and well-informed beliefs and values, even if not our own.

Perhaps, most important, teaching is a human relationship involving need, ability, and commitment. Our students need intellectual and moral growth. We are able to address their need. We join together in a commitment to do so. Students trust us to put their interest ahead of our own or the university's. We are privileged to receive that trust and commit to honoring it. Teaching, so understood, is a profession, an activity in which specialized knowledge is applied in the service of others with the aim of helping them live a good life. We are dedicated not only to the ends usually cited, the search for truth and the communication of knowledge, but to the development of the human potential of individual persons. The process of education should ennoble both teachers and students.

As you know, the lesson that we teach people is often overlooked. Such is the case in graduate education where we prepare the next generation of professors. If any form of professionalism is emphasized there, it remains discipline focused. Graduate students are encouraged to think of themselves as professional philosophers, mathematicians, and the like. One's profession is simply one's academic discipline. One's professional commitment is to advance the status of the discipline and one's place in it. Teaching is just a way to support that professional activity. Your example reminds me such a viewpoint is defective.

Even when not overlooked, the lesson that we teach people can be difficult to heed. To promote cost-saving efficiency and flexibility, universities are replacing tenured faculty with adjuncts, who are often underpaid, labor under heavy teaching loads, receive little to no employment benefits, and work from one short-term contract to the next. They have little time or energy to devote to their students and may even lack an office in which to meet them.

University administrators increasingly emphasize the numerical indicators of an efficient production machine: admission, retention, and graduation rates; costs of production; income from tuition, grants, and development. Scant attention is paid to educational quality.

Students are increasingly treated as customers. By their sophomore year in high school, they are deluged with glossy recruitment brochures, emphasizing a vision of their future selves defined by financial success in a chosen career. The marketing continues after they enroll. Departments compete for majors, with a message focused on economic concerns, never touching on other measures of human fulfillment or a broader conception of a good life. Treated from the start as customers, many students settle into that role. They fail to recognize that their humanity is being ignored.

As the university treats students as consumers and students see themselves as such, it is easy to get caught in the riptide. We see ourselves as employees and our students as mere third-party beneficiaries of our work for the university. We believe we are satisfying their interests by satisfying our own. Whether our teaching increases their ability to live a good life is not our concern. What matters is that they leave the university as satisfied customers, diploma or certificate in hand, ready to recommend the institution to others. A devil's bargain slithers into our relationship. We won't demand more of our students than their sense of satisfaction requires; they won't ask much from us, leaving plenty of time for our other pursuits. No longer united in the common cause of a genuine education, we leave one another alone.

When I was in my first year as an assistant professor, a senior colleague advised me not to bother learning the names of my students because doing so wasn't worth the trouble. After all, one group would soon be replaced by another. Your example helped me to see otherwise. Our students, and indeed colleagues and school, may not recognize what higher education is about, but in our teaching we should work to undermine their misconception. Doing so may place us at odds with our colleagues but will make for a rewarding life.

These are the lessons you taught me, Bob, and they have been the best and most sustaining of my academic career.

11

Happiness as Life Satisfaction

CHRISTINE VITRANO

Christine Vitrano is Professor of Philosophy at Brooklyn College of the City University of New York.

I TRANSFERRED TO NYU as a sophomore and kept hearing raves about Professor Gurland. Eventually I enrolled in one of his courses, and when I came to the first class, I found the large room filled with students, some even sitting on the floor because all the seats were taken. Yet as soon as the professor entered, the crowd became silent and awaited the lecture.

How engaging were his talks, always enlightening and peppered with funny stories filled with life lessons, many of which I still remember. His style cannot be replicated, but his aim to involve us all has influenced my own approach to teaching.

Bob brought happiness to many, and as it happens, my own research has focused on the concept of happiness. Let me then share some thoughts on the subject.

Two opposing perspectives of happiness dominate the literature: one equates happiness with virtue, the other with pleasure. The first is associated with Aristotle, who viewed happiness as the greatest good, something that had to be earned through living an exemplary life. According to Aristotle, happiness required achieving excellence in both your intellect and moral character, and although Aristotle recognized that a happy person is deeply satisfied with her life, he also thought that we could be mistaken about our own happiness. On Aristotle's view, if a person does not live up to the high standard of being morally and intellectually virtuous, then regardless of how satisfied she is with her life, she will fail to be happy.

In contrast to the Aristotelian view, hedonism identifies happiness with pleasure. This view was endorsed by Jeremy Bentham and John Stuart Mill but is also frequently found in the social sciences. Although the concept of pleasure has been a source of debate within philosophy, the consensus is that feelings of pleasure are identified not by a particular feeling but by the favorable attitude we take towards them, finding them enjoyable and wishing them to continue. Thus, according to the hedonist, happiness can be reduced to enjoyable experiences, and people are not mistaken about their own satisfaction.

These two views of happiness, whether as virtue or pleasure, are both right in one respect but wrong in another. The Aristotelian requires that you fully develop your moral and intellectual capacities to be deemed happy, yet a person living an entirely satisfied life may not meet the Aristotelian criterion for happiness. On the other hand, hedonism recognizes the importance of the individual's satisfaction, yet sometimes indulging in pleasure leads to unhappiness, as, for example, eating so much chocolate cake that it makes you sick.

My view, developed in my book *The Nature and Value of Happiness* (Westview Press, 2014) is that we ought to equate happiness with life satisfaction. In other words, a person is happy to the extent that she is satisfied with her life, and the more favorable her outlook, the happier she is. Thus, no constraints are placed on the source of one's satisfaction. Although I agree with the Aristotelian view that engaging in moral behavior is a crucial part of living well, I believe happiness is an independent concept not necessarily connected to morality, so judging a person happy implies nothing about the state of her character.

Although the life satisfaction view allows for the possibility of happiness in the absence of morality, it does not imply the two are mutually exclusive, and for many of us, being moral is an important source of satisfaction. For instance, if you value being a good parent, coworker, spouse, or friend, each of these roles will present moral obligations you will try to meet in order to be happy.

How does this discussion relate to Bob? He is a happy person, who finds deep satisfaction with his life, especially when he is meeting the moral obligations of a teacher, guiding those for whom he is responsible. Indeed, I believe students are drawn to him because he enjoys sharing his happiness by communicating his passion for ideas and offering wise counsel.

While other professors may take satisfaction in how many articles they have published, Bob judges his life by how many students he has helped. For him, teaching is not a burden but a blessing. And how fortunate are the many of us who have been the beneficiaries of his concern.

12

Military Disobedience

DAVID LUTZ

David Lutz is Professor of Philosophy at Holy Cross College in Notre Dame, Indiana.

BOB: I AM PRIVILEGED to have been one of your students while you were a visiting professor at the United States Military Academy. I will always be grateful to you for opening my mind to the possibility of using reason to find answers to many of life's most important questions. I am thankful for your penetrating yet charitable comments on my first attempts to write philosophical essays and for encouraging me to pursue graduate studies in philosophy after completing my military service. I also especially appreciate your being so generous with your time, corresponding with me for several years after I graduated from West Point. I can only guess how many thousands of hours during your illustrious teaching career you devoted to guiding your students. You changed the lives of so many because people have always been your highest priority. I am fortunate to have been one of them.

Although many regard philosophy as irrelevant to the real world, the subject centers on what kind of life one should live. No study could be more relevant to our lives. Unfortunately, wars and threats of wars are part of our lives. Thus, like Cincinnatus, who left his plow to lead the defense of his country and then returned to his farm, you temporarily left Greenwich Village and went up the Hudson to serve a tour of duty at the U.S. Military Academy. In the spring of 1978, your final semester at West Point and also mine, I had the good fortune to be your student in two courses: "Freud, Marx, Einstein" and "War and Morality." While I learned much in both, I would like to focus on an issue discussed in the latter, which was an elective course but should have been required for all cadets.

Suppose the President of the United States were to order the armed forces to fight a war that, in the professional judgment of the nation's highest-ranking military officers, would be unjust. What should those officers do?

In the case of My Lai, Vietnam, by nearly universal agreement, the soldiers of Lieutenant William Calley's platoon were obligated not to obey the order of their platoon leader to execute several hundred civilians. The Nuremberg Defense—"I was just following orders"—has no place in such a situation. The same is true if the superior is the Commander in Chief and the subordinates are generals and admirals.

If everything unethical were also illegal, a distinction between illegal and unethical orders would be unnecessary. Many unethical actions are legal, however, and we must distinguish obedience to unethical orders from obedience to illegal orders. Though by widespread agreement, senior officers should not obey illegal orders, even if they are issued by the Commander in Chief, such is not true of unethical orders. The consensus is that all legal orders, even if immoral, should be obeyed. For example, General (Retired) Richard B. Myers, who served as Chairman of the Joint Chiefs of Staff from 2001 to 2005, and military historian Richard H. Kohn cite moral disagreement as a reason military officers should not respond to orders they believe to be unethical by submitting their resignations:

> One individual's definition of what is moral, ethical, and even professional can differ from someone else's. There is

> no tradition of military resignation in the United States, no precedent—and for good reason. Even the hint of resignation would encourage civilians to choose officers more for compliance and loyalty than for competence, experience, intelligence, candor, moral courage, professionalism, integrity, and character.[1]

This explanation is puzzling. If morality were subjective, how would we know that competence is better than incompetence, integrity better than hypocrisy, or courage better than cowardice? If certain virtues, including moral courage, should be considered in deciding which officers should serve at the highest levels of leadership, then significant moral agreement exists. Why would we want to promote officers with moral courage and then forbid them to disobey immoral orders? Would not such refusal, at the cost of their military careers, be a heroic act of moral courage?

While different people define morality differently, it does not follow that there is no objective moral truth. If we have a genuine disagreement, there has to be some truth about which we are disagreeing. If moral disagreement means that we cannot attain knowledge of moral truth, just war theory would be pointless. But we can make correct judgments about which wars were, are, or would be just or unjust. Nevertheless, there is broad consensus that senior military officers should exercise their professional judgment only in deciding *how* wars should be fought, not *whether* they should be fought: "Civilian-elected officials oversee the larger strategic interests of the country, including the decision of when to deploy the military, while the armed forces make operational and tactical decisions if the military is called to action."[2]

That claim cannot be correct. Initiating an unjust war is a grave matter. Innocent civilians will die. If the opposing army is fighting a just war, its soldiers are also innocent. Military officers

1. Richard B. Myers and Richard H. Kohn, "The Military's Place," Foreign Affairs 86, no. 5 (2007), 149.

2. Patrick Paterson, "Civil-Military Relations: Guidelines in Politically Charged Societies," Parameters: The United States Army War College Quarterly 52, no. 1 (2022), 8.

have a responsibility of obedience to their civilian superiors but also a responsibility to their subordinates in a manner consistent with the moral tradition of their profession. The senior officer who obeys an order to start an unjust war puts his subordinates in the position of having to decide whether the war is just, and if they understand it to be unjust, whether to participate in an unjust war or face the consequences of refusing to do so. Shifting that responsibility downward would be a failure of senior leadership.

In military ethics far more attention is paid to the ethics of killing than the ethics of dying. Although virtuous soldiers do not hesitate to risk the sacrifice of their lives for a just cause, asking them to die for an unjust cause is unethical. Thus, obeying an order to start an unjust war is unjust, even if the order is given by the Commander in Chief.

The principle of civilian control of the military is important, but so is the principle that unjust wars should not be fought. Doing something wrong is wrong even if someone tells you to do it. Deciding not to obey an order of a civilian superior to start an unjust war and explaining the reason behind that choice would not pose a threat to civilian control of the military. If the noncommissioned officers in William Calley's platoon had decided not to obey his order to execute non-combatants, that refusal would not have challenged the principle that sergeants are subordinate to lieutenants and must obey their legal, ethical orders.

In sum, all military officers are obligated not to obey both illegal orders and unethical orders, even if the person giving the order is the President of the United States. Acknowledging this truth is important because scant evidence exists that recent presidents and their advisors have considered just war theory when making a decision to go to war.

Let me emphasize that I am not suggesting that senior military officers are free to disobey any order with which they disagree. I am only addressing the situation of an order by a civilian superior to start what would be, in the considered professional judgment of a senior military officer, an unjust war. Whether there may be other situations in which officers should not obey orders of their civilian superiors is a question for another day.

My reflections on these matters were stimulated by your extraordinary course. And when you left West Point and returned to NYU, the Academy's loss was NYU's gain.

Yet your influence on me continued. Just as you invested more of your time guiding your students than accumulating publications, I have followed your example. I am at a teaching college where I offer four courses every semester. I also taught for a decade in Africa (Kenya, Uganda, Nigeria), offering up to twelve courses a year. And some of my students, your philosophical grandchildren, have told me that my courses were life-changing for them—as yours were for me. Thus will future generations continue to be the beneficiary of your generosity.

PART III

WRITINGS

13

The Challenge of College Teaching

Robert H. Gurland

This essay is excerpted with minor changes from Bob Gurland's essay "Teaching Mathematics," Scholars Who Teach: The Art of College Teaching, ed. Steven M. Cahn (1978; Eugene, OR: Wipf and Stock Publishers, 2004).

Given that the three key issues in any course are who is to be taught, what is to be taught, and how the material is to be taught, I maintain that the what and how should be answered in terms of the who. The purpose of education is to communicate content to persons; we educate people. To ignore the recipient in favor of dedication to a subject creates the deadly environment that prevails in so many college classrooms today.

The alienation of students that results from a failure to place their role in proper perspective has become characteristic of higher education. This shortcoming is neither oversight nor accident. Rather, its roots lie in the philosophical position that regards the college and university as the playground of the faculty, an academic community formed for the purpose of affording professors the opportunity to pursue their scholarly interests within a milieu which provides all that is necessary for success, including libraries, contact with other interested scholars, subsidized attendance at scholarly conventions, light workloads, and sabbatical leaves. Such a view often results in the relegation of teaching responsibilities to secondary status. The students are then treated as a necessary evil, their presence on campus merely providing the financial wherewithal to allow the institution to sustain itself and permit faculty members to "do their own thing," a "thing" that all too often fails to include an attempt to improve teaching techniques.

The college community expends little constructive effort toward raising the level of classroom communication. Whereas great care has been given to the preparation of the prospective elementary or secondary school teacher, no wide-scale attempt has been made to ensure that a neophyte college instructor is capable of consistently offering a high level of classroom instruction. This tendency to eschew any systematic program for the heightening of teaching competence on the college level by instituting apprenticeship programs or developing seminars concerned with methodology seems to follow from treating two theses as axiomatic: (1) good teachers are born, not made; and (2) if individuals have demonstrated academic competence in a subject area, then necessarily they will be successful in communicating their knowledge in the classroom.

Although pedagogic skill is to a degree a function of the teacher's personality, wit, dynamism, and ability to relate to groups of students, nonetheless central skills in effective instruction, such as the selection of appropriate motivational devices and examples, employment of sound methodology, thoughtful apportionment of classroom time, anticipation of student difficulties, and competent testing and evaluation, can be acquired and should not be regarded as innate. Similarly, although knowledge of the material on the instructor's part is necessary, it is not sufficient because teaching involves a mastery of communication skills that are independent of most academic disciplines.

The problem of inadequate teaching is also the responsibility of administrators. Typically, their policy has been to award faculty members promotion and tenure primarily on the basis of research and publications, thus encouraging the faculty to concentrate on these activities at the expense of their teaching duties. Instead, professors should be urged to generate enthusiasm in the classroom while respecting the integrity of their subjects and recognizing the needs, attitudes, and dignity of their students. Those faculty who meet this challenge of college teaching should be duly recognized.

14

Aphorisms

Robert H. Gurland

#1

Time is the currency of love.

#2

Don't build your life around your wounds.

#3

Dying is easy, but living is hard.

#4

We are all subject to the tyranny of the clock.

#5

Don't mortgage the present for a future you may never have.

#6

You shouldn't spend your time and energy trying to get even.

#7

If you have no scars, you never left home.

#8

Societal visions stem from the visions of individuals.

#9

Life should imitate dreams.

#10

The culture of celebrity creates a sense of false intimacy.

#11

Don't be complicit in your own deterioration.

#12

A life is forged on the anvil of time.

#13

An infinite number of possible futures are rooted in the soil of the present.

#14

The narrative of a life is written a day at a time.

#15

Whereas the challenge for the young is to manage desire, the challenge for the aging is to manage loss.

#16

You leave this planet with an empty suitcase. What remains are the threads woven into the tapestry of the lives you have touched.

#17

The book of life is not judged by how voluminous it is but by its moral quality.

#18

Don't believe that nice guys finish last.

#19

Saints are in short supply.

#20

Life is like baseball. When at bat, don't get cheated. Get your good swings. When on the mound, go with your best stuff. Let it be that you have played well and have no regrets.

www.ingramcontent.com/pod-product-compliance
Lightning Source LLC
LaVergne TN
LVHW010035160826
845671LV00003B/141